THE
CHRISTIAN SABBATH

Terry L. Johnson

THE BANNER OF TRUTH TRUST

THE BANNER OF TRUTH TRUST

Head Office
3 Murrayfield Road
Edinburgh, EH12 6EL
UK

North America Office
PO Box 621
Carlisle, PA 17013
USA

banneroftruth.org

© The Banner of Truth Trust 2021
First published 2021

*

ISBN
Print: 978 1 80040 035 1
Epub: 978 1 80040 036 8
Kindle: 978 1 80040 037 5

*

Typeset in 10.5/13.5 pt Adobe Garamond Pro at
The Banner of Truth Trust

Printed in the USA by
VersaPress, Inc.,
East Peoria, IL.

CONTENTS

Introduction   5

Made for Man—Mark 2:23-28   15

Lord of the Sabbath—Mark 2:28-3:5   29

Practical Recommendations   43

Conclusion   49

The Sabbath and Delight—George Swinnock   55

Select Bibliography   57

INTRODUCTION

My childhood was lived in an America that largely was Sabbath-keeping. Sunday was a sacred day: the stores were closed, youth sports didn't hold practices or games, non-religious activities were discouraged. Professional sports had made inroads (though not until 1930s did the cities of Pittsburgh and Philadelphia allow their teams to play). Yet high school and college athletics avoided Sunday altogether. Some restaurants were open and even serious Christians had begun to patronise them. However, dining out was seen as an exception to the rule. Sabbath observance was the norm in North America from Dale's Code in Jamestown (1612) until the mid-1960s. 'Blue laws' kept the bars and stores closed, prevented the sale of liquor and restricted recreation and travel. Careful Sabbath observance was the norm for three and a half centuries from Maine to California and across all Protestant denominational lines: Episcopal, Methodist, Baptist, Congregational, Pentecostal, Lutheran, Reformed, and Presbyterian.

However, by the late 1960s the Sunday Sabbath had collapsed. The growing popularity of Sunday sports and shopping malls along with youth activities spelled its doom. Most of the blue laws have been repealed. Today only a tiny minority of Christians observe the Sabbath in any meaningful way. Methodist Bishop Arthur Moore (1888–1974) observed that his grandfather's generation referred to Sunday as the 'holy Sabbath,' his father's to the 'Sabbath,' and his to 'Sunday.' Today we think of it as the back half of the 'weekend.' This may be the commandment most visibly ignored and overtly violated by professed Bible-believing Christians today. Everywhere we look, the stores, the restaurants, the beaches, the stadiums, the golf courses, are open and full, and Christians are found in them all.

Previous generations of Christians saw things differently. The Christian Sabbath was understood to be the 'market day' or 'harvest day' of the soul.[1] Jonathan Edwards refers to the first day of the week, Sunday Sabbath, as 'the universal custom of the Christian church in all ages.'[2] A number of commentators have cited the Sunday Sabbath affirmations of early church fathers such as Ignatius, Irenaeus, Justin Martyr, Tertullian, Clement of Alexandria, Basil, Jerome, Augustine, and Eusebius of Caesarea, as well as the Council of Laodicea (AD 363). While it was common for the fathers to speak of the end of the Jewish Sabbath, none ever denied the continued authority of the fourth commandment which they identified with the Lord's Day, insisting upon a cessation from secular labour and the devotion of the whole day to public worship and private devotional exercises.[3] Still today the Romance languages refer to Sunday not as the day of the Sun, but *Domingo* (Spanish), *Dimanche* (French) and *Domenica* (Italian), the Lord's Day.

The leading spokesmen of Reformed Protestantism from the time of the Reformation to the Puritans of England in the seventeenth

[1] See James T. Dennison, *The Market Day of the Soul: The Puritan Doctrine of the Sabbath in England, 1532–1700* (Grand Rapids: Reformation Heritage Books, 2008); Thomas Brooks, 'London's Lamentations,' *The Works of Thomas Brooks* (Edinburgh: Banner of Truth Trust, 1980), I:288; Matthew Henry, 'A Serious Address to Those that Profane the Lord's Day,' in *The Complete Works of Matthew Henry* (1855; Grand Rapids: Baker Books, 1979), I:132.

[2] Jonathan Edwards, 'Perpetuity and Change of the Sabbath,' Sermon XIV, in *The Works of Jonathan Edwards* (Edinburgh: Banner of Truth Trust, 1974), II:100.

[3] See Thomas Watson, *The Ten Commandments* (1692, 1890; London: Banner of Truth Trust, 1965), 117; R. L. Dabney, 'The Christian Sabbath: Its Nature, Design and Proper Observance,' in *Discussions: Evangelical and Theological* (1892; London: Banner of Truth Trust, 1967), I:358-59. For similar citations from a more recent publication, see Roger T. Beckwith and Wilfrid Stott, *The Christian Sunday: A Biblical and Historical Study* (Grand Rapids: Baker Book House, 1980).

century (e.g. John Owen, Thomas Manton, Richard Baxter, etc.), to the Puritans of New England in the eighteenth century (e.g. Thomas Shepard, Cotton Mather, Jonathan Edwards), to the Princeton theologians of the nineteenth and early twentieth century (e.g. Charles Hodge, B. B. Warfield, Geerhardus Vos), to the Westminster theologians of the mid to late twentieth century (e.g. J. Gresham Machen, Cornelius Van Til, John Murray), all were strong advocates of the Christian Sabbath. Prior to the mid-twentieth century, one would be hard pressed to find even a single mainstream evangelical teacher, whether D. L. Moody (1837–99), C. H. Spurgeon (1834–92), J. C. Ryle (1816–1900), Donald Grey Barnhouse (1895–1960), or Martyn Lloyd-Jones (1899–1981), who wasn't. 'Dad, no one agrees with you about this,' my children have been wont to say. For most of 2,000 years, or at least most of the last 500 years, I would answer, no one *disagreed* with me.[4]

Among the Reformed, Sabbath observance achieved confessional status with the *Heidelberg Catechism* (1563), the *Westminster Confession of Faith* (1648), the *Savoy Declaration* (Congregational, 1658), and the *London Confession* (Baptist, 1689). Even Luther, in his *Larger Catechism* (Sections 88-100), argues for a 'strict observance' of the fourth commandment, one 'occupied with heavenly things.' When the older authors listed the sins or 'profane courses' of the unconverted, they would include lying, swearing, stealing, uncleanness (sexual sin), all sins that are obvious to us, and to our surprise today, Sabbath-breaking.[5] The latter was taken with utmost seriousness. When they wrote on the subject, they often did massively, as can be seen in the reprints of Nicholas Bound's (1551–1613)

[4] Brooks: 'This hath been the judgment of most judicious divines in all ages' ('London's Lamentations,' *Works*, VI:300).

[5] E.g. Thomas Boston, *Human Nature in its Fourfold State* (1720; London: Banner of Truth Trust, 1964), 269.

The True Doctrine of the Sabbath,[6] the text of which runs 446 pages, and Thomas Shepherd's (1605–49) *Theses Sabbaticae*, which covers 271 pages of tiny print,[7] and John Owen's *Exercitations Concerning… Day of Sacred Rest*, nearly 300 pages in the nineteenth volume of his *Works*.[8]

There is an old saying in the Jewish community: The Jews didn't keep the Sabbath, the Sabbath kept the Jews. Similarly, it commonly was believed that the loss of the Sunday Sabbath would spell disaster for the survival of Christianity. 'It is not too much to say,' J. C. Ryle warned, 'that the prosperity or decay of English Christianity depends on the maintenance of the Christian Sabbath.'[9] Southern Presbyterian R. L. Dabney (1820–98) maintained that it was a historic fact 'that the vitality and holiness of the church are usually in proportion to its reverence for the Sabbath.'[10]

Previous generations of Christians fiercely resisted the erosion of careful Sunday Sabbath observance. When the first Glasgow to Edinburgh train ran on Sunday, March 13, 1842, it was greeted in

[6] Nicholas Bound, *The True Doctrine of the Sabbath* (1595; Grand Rapids and Dallas, TX: Naphtali Press and Reformation Heritage Books, 2015).

[7] Thomas Shepard, *Theses Sabbaticae*, Vol. 3 of the *Works of Thomas Shepard* (1853; Ligonier: Soli Deo Gloria, 1992).

[8] John Owen, 'Exercitations Concerning the Name, Origin, Nature, Use, and Continuance of a Day of Sacred Rest, in *An Exposition of the Epistle to the Hebrews*, Volume II (1855; Grand Rapids: Baker Books, 1980).

[9] J. C. Ryle, 'The Christian Sabbath,' in *Knots Untied: being Plain Statements on Disputed Points in Religion from an Evangelical Standpoint* (Edinburgh: Banner of Truth Trust, 2016), 334. He goes on to say, 'Take away a man's Sabbath and his religion soon comes to nothing' (343); see also Henry: 'It is so necessary, that revealed religion, and with it all religion, would in all probability have been lost … if it had not been kept up by the observation of sabbaths' ('Serious Address,' in *Works,* I:118-19).

[10] Dabney, 'Christian Sabbath,' *Discussions*, I:541. He also argues 'that the proper observance of the Sabbath is a bulwark of practical Christianity' (496), even 'where there is no Sabbath there is at last no Christianity' (508).

Edinburgh by 'a threatening battery' of angry Scottish Presbyterian clergymen warning disembarking passengers that they had bought 'tickets to hell!' The saintly Robert Murray M'Cheyne, among others, mourned the loss of Scotland's Sabbath quiet and bitterly denounced the running of the trains. The Glasgow Presbytery called it 'a grievous outrage on the religious feelings of the people of Scotland.'[11] The 'Bullocks' department store, the last of the large department stores in Southern California to open its doors on Sunday in the mid-1960s, felt the need to run full-page ads in the *Los Angeles Times* lamenting Sunday openings and the loss of revenue to competitors, which was forcing them to finally give up and give in.

The Lord's Day was 'the day of days' for our spiritual ancestors. The Puritan George Swinnock (1627–73) called it 'the golden spot of the week,' the 'daybreak of eternal brightness,' the 'queen of days,' the 'crown of time,' the 'epitome of heaven,' even 'heaven in a glass.'[12] Today it is just another day of the week. Today few give any special status to Sunday at all. One writer recalls how different it was for her in her childhood and youth. Her world was the world in which many of us were raised. She reminisced:

> One Sunday morning during Sunday School we talked about whether or not a farmer could walk around his farm on Sunday. Our elder-teacher thought it would be a risky thing to do, since the farmer would probably think about how he could improve his corn yield or what repairs he should make to his barn. That would be 'working,' and it was sinful to work on Sunday. If the

---

[11] See account in William Barclay, *The Ten Commandments for Today* (Grand Rapids: William B. Eerdmans Publishing Co., 1973), 43.

[12] George Swinnock, 'The Christian Man's Calling,' in *The Works of George Swinnock* (1868: Edinburgh: Banner of Truth Trust, 1992), I:258-60; James Durham calls it 'that sweet and desirable day' (*A Practical Exposition of the Ten Commandments* [1675; Dallas: Naphtali Press and Grand Rapids: Reformation Heritage Books, 2018]), 218.

farmer could take a walk and think about how God created the earth, it would be alright.

That's the kind of discussion we had in 1959. Can you imagine that kind of discussion today, when churches have had to let out by noon sharp so members can get home in time for pro football on their T.V.s? Would anybody today understand the spiritual wrestling we went through over the question of whether or not our children could go to birthday parties on Sunday? The newspaper was not opened until after evening service …

Around here our family is regarded as being somewhat quaint because we don't watch T.V., shop, or eat in restaurants on Sunday. I have learned to say, 'I don't believe it's right for me,' so I do not impose my Sabbath-keeping on anyone else. Such imposition is wrong, I have been told, since each Christian must be led by the Holy Spirit to keep the fourth Commandment in his and her own way. Since we cannot accuse the Holy Spirit of being inconsistent, we deduce that he likes variety! Anyway, the argument goes, it is not what we do not do that keeps the Sabbath, but what is in our hearts, and only God can see the heart. Dare I judge the man who goes to a baseball game on Sunday is not loving God while he eats his hot dog and drinks his beer? …

It's all so confusing! The rules keep changing, and I end up being either legalistic or old-fashioned, but never right.[13]

By the 1970s my own memory of my childhood Sabbath had vanished. As a college student I discovered a wonderful Christian book store where, as an eager, growing Christian, I used to spend hours browsing. One Saturday I called to see if it had a particular book (it did) and if I could drop in on Sunday after church and purchase it. They explained that they were closed on Sunday and

[13] Jean Shaw, 'Six Flags Instead of Sunday School,' *Presbyterian Journal,* May 24, 1984.

then added this somewhat accusatory question, 'Don't you think we need to rest on the Lord's Day too?' I was taken aback by the question, and then offended. My first thought was, 'What a bunch of legalists.' The truth of the matter was I had long abandoned any consideration of resting on Sunday. Once I got over their affront to my imagined liberated Christian practice (of non-resting), I forgot again about the concept of a Christian Sabbath.

Even secular observers have expressed surprise at the ease of the Christian community's concessions to the world. Years ago Rick Reilly, at the time the gifted *Sports Illustrated* columnist, wrote an article entitled 'Let us ~~Pray~~ Play.' He complained, 'Sports has nearly swallowed Sunday whole.' Who is to blame? 'The first people (we) might want to crack down on are the Christians themselves,' he insisted. He quoted Rich Cizik of the National Association of Evangelicals, who told his son's coach that he would not be available to play on Sundays. The coach looked shocked. Cizik said, 'You act like nobody's ever said that to you before.' He answered, 'Honestly? They haven't.' Noting that a mere handful of clergy had complained, Reilly concluded his article:

> I'm with the holy men … I just feel sorry for these kids who get nothing but organized sports crammed down their gullets 24/7. Even God took a day off.
>
> Kids might weep with joy to get a day off from sports. If they don't spend it at church, maybe they'll spend it getting to know their siblings' names again. Or swing in a hammock without a coach screaming, 'Get your hips into it, Samantha!'
>
> Hey, you do what you want. Just remember, when little Shaniqua has two free throws to win or lose a game on some Sunday morning, good luck finding somebody who'll answer your prayers.[14]

[14] Rick Reilly, 'Let Us ~~Pray~~ Play,' *Sports Illustrated*, April 26, 2004.

Not until well into my studies in seminary in England did I begin seriously to consider what was appropriate activity on Sunday. To my surprise, nearly everyone in Bristol, England in the late 1970s seemed to rest on Sunday. The shops were closed, or at least most of them. Even typically unbelieving university students seemed to lay aside their studies. The Christian customs of previous generations continued to influence the now pagan British masses. Prompted by their example, I began to examine the question for myself. What was I to do on Sunday? Was I to put down my books and enjoy a Sabbath rest? Was I to attend morning and evening worship services and spend the rest of the day doing what further enhanced my love and appreciation for God and his works? Was I to read Christian books, the Bible, enjoy nature, pray, and have discussions concerning the things of God? These are the kinds of spiritual disciplines for which the Sabbath allegedly was designed to provide time. Or was I to treat Sunday like every other day, except to attend church in the morning and perhaps in the evening as well?

Given the general confusion on the Sabbath question today, we want to examine what the Bible has to say, beginning with Jesus' conflict with the religious authorities over what is and is not permitted, and reaching back to opening chapters of Genesis. We admit, as we do so, to bringing a certain bias to the question. It seems to us that it is more than a bit arbitrary to say that the other nine commandments apply today: prohibitions of other gods, images, abusing God's name, dishonouring parents, murder, adultery, theft, false witness, and coveting. They are all forbidden; all of them. It seems to us both arbitrary and self-serving ('strange and absurd,' according to James Durham) then to reach into the middle of the 'Ten Words' (Deut. 10:4) and extract the fourth commandment and claim that it no longer applies, or claim that its careful observance is a form of legalism. [15] The fourth commandment, like the other nine and unlike any other commands, was written by God's own finger, underscoring their central importance, on tablets of stone, a powerful representation of their permanence. [16] Like the other nine, it is moral, 'purely moral' as Watson claims. [17]

The New Testament does not treat how we observe the Sabbath as a minor issue. Each of the three Synoptic Gospels presents the confrontation with Pharisees plucking heads of grain on the Sabbath (Mark 2:23-28; Matt. 12:1-8; Luke 6:1-5), the healing of the man with a withered hand (Mark 3:1-6; Matt. 12:9-14; Luke 6:6-11), and the healing of the woman who was 'bent over' (Luke 13:10-17). To these the Gospel of John adds the healing at the pool at Bethesda (John 5:1-8) and the healing of the man born blind (John 9:1-41). Having been delivered over to the Babylonians for their Sabbath-breaking (e.g. Isa. 56:1-8; Jer. 17:19-27; Ezek. 20:19-27), and determined not to repeat that error, devout contemporaries of Jesus went to the other extreme, unreasonably and cruelly restricting Sabbath activity. This imbalance Jesus corrects by doing good and saving lives on the Sabbath. He thereby restores the principle that the Sabbath command was given for man, while he retains his lordship over it.

[15] Durham, *Ten Commandments*, 155. He insists that if the fourth commandment were not moral and perpetual, 'a reason would be given why among the ten, one and only one is set down, so far different from the rest' (157).

[16] The durability of the stones 'was to represent the perpetual obligation of all that was written on them' (Dabney, 'Christian Sabbath,' *Discussions*, I:505; cf I:523); see also Thomas Boston, *A Commentary on the Shorter Catechism* (1773, 1853; Edmonton, Canada: Still Water Revival Books, 1993), II:189; Edwards, 'Perpetuity and Change,' Sermon XIII, *Works*, II:95.

[17] Watson, *Ten Commandments*, 94; Shepard goes to great lengths to establish the moral nature of the 4th commandment (see Shepard, *Theses Sabbaticae*, 28-186), as does John Owen, 'Exercitations Concerning a Day of Sacred Rest,' *Hebrews*, II:326-85; cf Durham, *Ten Commandments*, 155-57; Boston, *Shorter Catechism*, II:188-89; Edwards, 'Perpetuity and Change,' Sermon XIII, *Works*, II:95-96.

Given the continuity between the Testaments, given Jesus' affirmation of the whole law (Matt. 5:17-20) and the apostle Paul's citation of multiple commandments as normative (Rom. 13:8-10; Eph. 6:1-3), we are predisposed to think that the fourth commandment is a moral law which still applies to believers today. Its careful observance is no more legalism than is obedience to the other nine.[18] Let us then look at these matters more closely.

[18] It may even be argued, based on the flow of 1 Timothy 1:8-11, that the apostle Paul has in mind commandments 4-9 as he progresses from the 'unholy and profane' (fourth commandment) to 'those who strike fathers and mothers' (fifth commandment), 'murders' (sixth commandment), to 'sexually immoral, men who practice homosexuality' (seventh commandment), 'enslavers' (eighth commandment), to 'liars, perjurers' (ninth commandment). See Sinclair B. Ferguson, *Devoted to God: Blueprints for Sanctification* (Edinburgh: Banner of Truth Trust, 2016), 262-63.

MADE FOR MAN

Mark 2:23-28

The frenetic pace of life in modern times is well attested. The world makes constant demands upon us to go and to do. The pace is exhausting and the interruptions constant. Electronic devices beep and chirp for our attention, demanding that we flit from one thing to the next. Time for rest, for meditation, for sustained thought, for contemplation of divine verities, for self-evaluation, for assessment of life, its meaning, its priorities, its direction, its termination, and eternity is squeezed out. The mould into which the modern world would squeeze us is superficial, obsessed with the immediate and the temporal, and destructive of spiritual life. Is there a divine provision to help us in this struggle for our souls? Indeed, there is: the weekly Sabbath. It's not the only provision. There are other important provisions. Yet the Sabbath is a crucial provision.[19]

As Jesus brings his initial conflict over the Sabbath with the Pharisees to a conclusion, he declares the first of the principles that guided his Sabbath teaching. 'And he said to them, "The Sabbath was made for man, not man for the Sabbath"' (Mark 2:27).

What is the origin of this Sabbath of which Jesus speaks? The Sabbath was 'made,' was instituted by God at creation, prior to the ceremonial law, prior to the fall, in paradise, and 'undoubtedly rooted in nature; in our human nature, and in the nature of the

[19] Thankful there is evidence of this, a growing awareness of the importance of Sabbath rest in surprising places: see John Mark Comer, *The Ruthless Eliminator of Hurry* (Colorado Springs: Water Brook, 2019).

created universe,' says the great Old Princeton theologian B. B. Warfield.[20] God created for six days and rested on the seventh. Like marriage and labour, the Sabbath is a creation ordinance instituted from the very beginning. When at Sinai God says, 'Remember,' it indicates, says Matthew Henry, 'that it was the revival of an old commandment, which had been forgotten.'[21] The foundation of the Sabbath is in Eden: 'So God blessed the seventh day and made it holy, because on it God rested from all his work that he had done in creation' (Gen. 2:3).

Why did God rest? He rested, not because he was tired or needed rest, but in order to provide a pattern for humanity.[22] Moses first reinstituted or revived the Sabbath command prior to Sinai: 'Tomorrow a day of solemn rest, a holy Sabbath to the Lord' (Exod. 16:23-28). The Sabbath, we repeat, was instituted before the ceremonial law.[23] What was instituted at creation, revived upon departure from Egypt, was then enshrined in the Decalogue, citing its roots in creation: 'For in six days the LORD made heaven and earth, the sea, and all that is in them, and rested on the seventh

[20] B. B. Warfield, 'The Foundations of the Sabbath in the Word of God,' in *Selected Shorter Writings of Benjamin B. Warfield,* Volumes 1 & 2, ed. John E. Meeter (Phillipsburg, NJ: Presbyterian and Reformed Publishing Company, 1970), 1:309. It is 'built into the very structure of the universe,' says former Yale Divinity School professor Brevard S. Childs (*The Book of Exodus: A Critical, Theological Commentary*), Old Testament Library (Philadelphia: The Westminster Press, 1974), 416.

[21] Henry, 'Serious Address,' *Works,* I:121; Ferguson, *Devoted to God,* 263; Durham, *Ten Commandments,* 179; Boston, *Commentary on the Shorter Catechism,* 2:188.

[22] 'What could be the meaning of God's resting the seventh day, and hallowing and blessing it, which he did, before giving of the fourth commandment, unless he hallowed and blessed it with respect to mankind?' asks Edwards ('Perpetuity and Change,' Sermon XIII, *Works,* II:95; cf Henry, 'Serious Address,' *Works,* I:21).

[23] See Boston, *Shorter Catechism*, II:188-91.

day. Therefore the LORD blessed the Sabbath day and made it holy' (Exod. 20:11).[24]

Humanity is to follow the divine example of rest each seventh day, 'an exceedingly weighty reason,' says Durham.[25] Jesus teaches, 'The Sabbath was made for *anthropon*,' (from which we get our word anthropology) for 'man,' not just for Israel or even the whole people of God, but for all humanity (the use of *dia*, 'for' plus the *accusative* of 'man' means 'on account of' or 'for the sake of'). In other words, the purpose of the Sabbath is to benefit the human race universally.[26] God 'blessed' the Sabbath. His blessing means that he is prepared to enrich and refresh all who observe it the ways that go above and beyond the blessings of other days of the week. He reserves distinctive benefits, both in kind and volume, in both the physical and spiritual realms for the observant.

'He made and still makes it useful and refreshing as a special blessing to his people,' Durham assures us.[27] 'He stands ready,' adds Edwards, 'then especially to hear prayers, to accept of religious services,

<hr />

[24] John Murray: 'God's mode of operation is the exemplar on the basis of which the sequence for man is patterned' (*Principles of Conduct,* [London: Tyndale Press, 1957], 32); The underlying principle, says Geerhardus Vos, is that 'man must copy God in his course of life' (*Biblical Theology* [Grand Rapids: Eerdmans Publishing Co., 1948], 155).

[25] Durham, *Ten Commandments*, 159; Boston: 'God's example proposed for imitation is a most binding one' (*Shorter Catechism*, II:201).

[26] Edwards: 'The command of God, that every seventh day should be devoted to religious exercises, is founded in the universal state and nature of mankind' ('Perpetuity and Change,' Sermon XIII, *Works*, II:95); Warfield: 'These commandments are but the positive publication to Israel of the universal human duties, the common morality of mankind' ('Foundations of the Sabbath,' in *Selected Writings*, I:312); J. C. Ryle: It is 'part of the eternal law of God … It is one of the everlasting rules which God has revealed for the guidance of all mankind' ('Christian Sabbath,' *Knots Untied*, 335).

[27] Durham, *Ten Commandments,* 159. Boston adds, 'It is a kindness that we are obliged to rest on the Lord's day. Our interest is our duty, and our duty is our interest' (*Shorter Catechism*, II:200).

to meet his people, to manifest himself to them, to give his Holy Spirit and blessing to those who diligently and conscientiously sanctify it.'[28]

How do we benefit by observing the Sabbath command?

Physical well-being

First, the Sabbath was given for our physical good. The actual language of the fourth commandment unfolds the details of Sabbath observance primarily in terms of physical rest and refreshment.

> Remember the Sabbath day, to keep it holy. Six days you shall labour, and do all your work, but the seventh day is a Sabbath to the LORD your God. On it you shall not do any work, you, or your son, or your daughter, your male servant, or your female servant, or your livestock, or the sojourner who is within your gates (Exod. 20:8-10).

This obligatory day of rest is a wonderful provision, a 'merciful appointment' in Ryle's words, of God for all humanity.[29] All common labour is to cease. A holy rest is to be observed. 'Six days,' and six days only, 'you shall labour' (Exod. 20:9; Deut. 5:13). On the Sabbath 'you shall not do any work' (Exod. 20:10; Deut. 5:14). God intended it 'for the repose of our bodies,' Henry explains, that we 'might rest, and not be tired out with the constant business of the world.'[30] God is mandating that we take a day-long break from our daily tasks once every seven days. One day in seven is to be wholly devoted to rest and refreshment for the sake of our health, happiness, and blessing. Businessmen and professionals are to close their briefcases; labourers

---

[28] Edwards, 'Perpetuity and Change,' Sermon XV, *Works*, II:102. Further, Edwards insists, 'If it be the day on which God requires us especially to seek him, we may argue, that it is a day on which especially he will be found ... a time wherein God especially loves to be sought, and loves to be found' (II:102).

[29] Ryle, 'Christian Sabbath,' *Knots Untied*, 341.

[30] Matthew Henry, *Exposition of the Old and New Testament* (1708–10; various editions), on Mark 3:27; also Ryle, 'Christian Sabbath,' *Knots Untied*, 342.

are to put down their tools; students are to close their books; cooks are to put down their pans. Yard work, house work, school work, office work can all wait for Monday to Saturday. All are to take a day-long break from the 24/7 world of ceaseless labour.

When I first began to observe a Sunday Sabbath as a student, I was encouraged by the impact it made on my work week. Students rarely escape the pressure of studying. What is true of students is true of most everyone. We can always be doing something more. Guilt feelings follow us wherever we go. A voice constantly whispers, 'You should be studying' or working or accomplishing something. We struggle with what has been called the 'tyranny of the urgent.' Nothing ever silenced the voice nagging me to get busy except a stronger voice, the command of God that I *must* rest.

Because of that stronger voice I adopted a new work pattern. I would work until the library closed Saturday night and then put down my books, refusing to pick them up until Monday morning. Doing so forced me to become more efficient in my use of the six days designated for labour, and I found that I was able to do in six days what previously was spread over seven days. And Sunday? Sunday became a sacred day of comprehensive peace and relaxation. I experienced complete rest: psychological, physical, and spiritual. As a result, I was refreshed and ready for work on Monday. This is the joy of Sabbath observance. God gave us a Sabbath day to liberate us from the tyranny of our busy labours, whether those of a student, a businessman, a shopkeeper, a professional, a labourer, or whatever. Our work can wait, and God insists that it does. 'You shall not do any work.'

Yet because the Sabbath rest is for 'man,' that is, all humanity, not just Christians, God is insisting that we promote the rest of others. 'You shall not do any work, you or your son or your daughter, your male or your female servant,' even your 'livestock' and the 'sojourner' (Exod. 20:10; Deut. 5:14). We are not to employ or hire others (even our children) to serve us on Sunday. All our economic transactions are to cease. If we shop, buy gasoline, frequent restaurants, watch athletic events, we are hiring people to serve us, wait on us, or entertain us, and thereby robbing them of the potential of Sabbath rest. Whether they want that rest or not is irrelevant. The *Westminster Confession of Faith* identifies (rightly, as we've seen) the Sabbath command as 'a positive, moral, and perpetual commandment binding all men in all ages' (XXI.7). They (the unbelieving and unobservant) are obligated to keep the Sabbath. *Our* obligation is not to hire them, and not to tempt them with the opportunity to work. The Sabbath forces us and helps those around us to slow down, and rest, and recuperate. It helps us establish a pattern of work and rest, to work efficiently, and to sort through our priorities. It is for our physical good. As the whole Christian community rests, store openings become less profitable on Sunday and many will choose to remain closed, thereby extending our rest to our unbelieving neighbours.

Spiritual well-being

Second, the Sabbath is for our spiritual well-being. Physical rest from ordinary labour is intended in its own right, yet it also serves a higher purpose. Secular activity is to be set aside in favour of spiritual activity. 'It was made for the profit and comfort of our souls,' says Edwards.[31] 'Remember' means commemorate or celebrate through religious observance. It is a memorial day, commemorating creation and redemption. The Sabbath command carves out a block of time for undisturbed focus on spiritual realities. The Sabbath was the day of the 'holy convocation,' of public worship in Israel (e.g. Lev. 23:3). Double the number of sacrifices were offered as were on ordinary days (Num. 28:9, 10).

[31] Edwards, 'Perpetuity and Change,' Sermon XV, *Works*, II:101; see also Durham, *Ten Commandments*, 179, 213.

A number of authors point out that the command is not 'remember the seventh day,' but 'remember the Sabbath.'[32] Because of the resurrection, post-resurrection appearances on the first day of the week (John 20:1, 19, 26), and the giving of the Holy Spirit on Pentecost (also the first day of the week—Acts 2), Sunday became the *Christian* Sabbath, the day on which the early church met (e.g. 1 Cor. 16:1, 2; Acts 20:7), also known as the Lord's Day (Rev. 1:10). The apostle Paul directed that collections were to be made on the 'first day of the week' (1 Cor. 16:1, 2). He designated the first day, an instruction that Ryle finds 'wholly inexplicable' if, as some maintain, 'the apostles kept no one day more holy than another.'[33] Why not just 'when you meet?' Why not a second, or third, or fourth day? That is what we might have expected if the day of worship were a matter of indifference. Instead, the apostle specifies the first day because it had been established as the day of Christian worship from the very beginning, a practice confirmed by the unanimous testimony of the church fathers.[34]

The Sabbath, then, was not merely or primarily for physical rest. It was to be 'hallowed,' or kept 'holy' and set apart from the rest of the week for godly ends (Exod. 20:8). We are to 'remember' (Exod. 20:8) or 'observe' (Deut. 5:12) the Sabbath through religious

[32] For example, Boston, *Shorter Catechism*, II:187; Durham, *Ten Commandments*, 184; Edwards, 'Perpetuity and Change,' Sermon XIII, *Works*, II:96, 97; Henry, 'Serious Address,' *Works*, I:121.

[33] Ryle, 'Christian Sabbath,' *Knots Untied*, 338; see also Durham, *Ten Commandments*, 183-207.

[34] Again, see Beckwith, *The Christian Sunday*; see also Boston, *Shorter Catechism*, II:192-93; Shepard, *Theses Sabbaticae*, 187-215; Flavel, 'An Exposition of the Assembly's Catechism,' *The Works of John Flavel* (1820; London: Banner of Truth Trust, 1968), VI:234; Owen provides an extended defence of the move of the Sabbath from the sixth to the first day of the week ('Exercitations Concerning a Day of Sacred Rest,' *Hebrews*, II:403-67); Edwards, 'Perpetuity and Change,' Sermon XLV, *Works*, II:96-100.

exercises. We are to celebrate and commemorate the great works of God in creation (highlighted in Exod. 20:11) and redemption (highlighted in Deut. 5:15).[35] Sunday, the first day of the week, is pre-eminently the day in which God's people assemble twice for worship, receive the spiritual refreshment that they need, and find rest for their souls.[36] Sunday is a 'sacred day,' says Swinnock (1627–73), expressing the classic view, spent altogether in 'sacred duties.'[37] This means that 'the business of the Sabbath is the greatest business of our lives,' says Edwards.[38] It is a day devoted to public worship, and also to family and private worship, Bible reading, the singing of praises, and godly conversations. It is to be set apart from all the other days of the week. It is to be devoted to worship and the things of God, and all other activities are to be set aside in order to fulfill this one end.

The students in my youth group in Coral Gables used to ask with unmasked frustration, 'So what do we do, go to church and then sit around and rest all day?' The answer is no. 'Though it be a day of rest,' Edwards explains, 'yet it was not designed to be a day of idleness.'[39] The people of God in heaven will have perfect rest yet they will not be inactive. Our rest is not merely a rest *from* but a rest

---

[35] Charles Hodge: 'If the deliverance of the Hebrew from the bondage in Egypt should be commemorated, how much more the redemption of the world by the Son of God. If the creation of the material universe should be kept in perpetual remembrance, how much more the new creation secured by the resurrection of Jesus Christ from the dead' (*Systematic Theology* [1870–73; Grand Rapids: Eerdmans Publishing Co., 1981], III:330).

[36] Henry: 'Those therefore undoubtedly profane the Lord's day, who absence themselves from the public worship of God, either the former or latter part of the day' ('Serious Address,' *Works*, I:119).

[37] Swinnock, 'Christian Man's Calling,' *Works*, I:361; Boston refers to 'holy exercises' (*Shorter Catechism*, II:186).

[38] Edwards, 'Perpetuity and Change of the Sabbath,' Sermon XV, *Works*, I:101.

[39] *Ibid.*, II:103. Both the *Larger Catechism* (Q. 119) and the *Shorter Catechism* (Q. 61) warn of 'profaning the day by idleness.'

for. It's a 'day of *holy rest,*' says Henry, 'in order to do *holy work.*'[40] 'Obviously, the Sabbath, in our Lord's view, was not a day of sheer idleness,' says Warfield in his comments on John 5:17 ('My Father is working until now, and I am working'). 'Inactivity was not its mark.'[41] Moreover, it is the Lord's *Day.* It is not the Lord's morning, or worse, the Lord's hour. It is a day upon which the Lord places his name. It is a *day,* not 12 hours or 18 hours or 23 hours, but a day, a *full* day, a period of 24 hours. 'The whole day is God's by *ordination,*' Swinnock asks, 'and why should it not be his by *observation?*'[42] A *whole* day is to be kept holy by participating in the worship services of the church and focusing our attention on the things of God throughout the rest of the day, undistracted 'all the day, from (our) own works, words, and thoughts about (our) worldly employments and recreations.' Rather, the day is to be 'taken up, *the whole time,* in the public and private exercises of his worship, and in the duties of necessity and mercy' (*WCF* XXI.8).[43]

[40] Henry, 'Serious Address,' *Works,* I:121 (emphasis added); Flavel: it is 'not a mere natural or civil, but an holy rest' ('Exposition,' *Works,* VI:235); also Boston, *Shorter Catechism,* II:196, 199.

[41] Warfield, 'Foundations of the Sabbath,' *Selected Writings,* I:317. He says further, 'Rest is not the true essence of the Sabbath, nor the end of its institution; it is the means to a further end, which constitutes the real Sabbath "rest." We are to rest from our own things that we may give ourselves to the things of God' (I:318); Commenting on Jesus' 'work' in John 5:17, John Murray argues that his Sabbath activity is 'consonant with the rest of the Sabbath precisely because the rest the Sabbath requires is *not the rest of inaction.* So rest is *not inactivity*; it is not unemployment, but employment of another sort from that of the six days' (*Principles of Conduct,* 33); also Murray, 'The Relevance of the Sabbath,' *Collected Writings,* I:227, 228.

[42] Swinnock, 'Christian Man Calling,' *Works,* I:245 (emphasis added); cf. Durham, *Ten Commandments,* 180; Boston, *Shorter Catechism,* II:189, 204; Shepard, *Theses Sabbaticae,* 72-73, 261; Flavel, 'Exposition,' *Works,* VI:234; Brooks, 'London's Lamentations,' *Works,* VI:299-300.

[43] See also *Larger Catechism* Questions 117, 119; *Shorter Catechism* Questions 60, 61.

Here is a question worth asking: Does God have a programme for spiritual growth? An informed Christian will say yes, we grow as the Holy Spirit takes what Christ has accomplished on the cross and applies it to us through the word, prayer, and the sacraments. These are the 'ordinary means of grace.' These are Christ's 'gospel ordinances.' Designating a day devoted to Christ and his ordinances is a *key component in this programme.* The older authors understood this. The Sabbath is 'a main foundation of godliness,' says Durham.[44] It is in a sense another of the gospel ordinances. There would be no reason for setting aside a day, as opposed to a partial day or a designated part of each day, if this were not the case. John Owen refers to the Christian Sabbath not as itself an ordinance *per se* (like the word, sacraments, and prayer), but as 'the sacred repository of all sanctifying ordinances.' Yet his meaning is the same. He denies that the Christian religion 'can be maintained without a due observation of a stated day of sacred rest.'[45] Thomas Case (1598–1682) identifies holiness as 'the great end for which God hath ordained a sabbath.' He defines it as 'a medium to make his people holy.'[46] Similarly, Thomas Brooks (1608–80) insists that 'the ends for which the Lord's day was appointed are all spiritual, viz. the glory of God, the illumination, conversion, and salvation of sinners, and the edification, confirmation, consolation of saints.'[47] The implication, it seems to us, is that

[44] Durham, *Ten Commandments*, 149; Shepard argues that a whole day is designated rather than a portion of each day because of the problem of sufficiently disentangling oneself from worldly concerns for 'some small piece of a day' (*Theses Sabbaticae*, 73).

[45] Owen, 'Exercitations Concerning a Day of Sacred Rest,' *Hebrews*, II:263, 264. Whether one sees the Sabbath as an ordinance or as a *compliment* to the ordinances, or perhaps even as the primary *context* in which the ordinances function, the role that it plays in the spiritual health of the people of God is vital.

[46] Thomas Case, 'Of Sabbath Sanctification,' *Puritan Sermons* (Wheaton, IL: Richard Owen Roberts Publishers, 1981), VI:40.

[47] Brooks, 'London's Lamentations,' *Works*, VI:296.

this provision is necessary if the spiritual life of God's people is to be sustained. Both in the Old Testament and New Testament the church as a whole and believers as individuals flourish as they gather together each Sabbath under the ministry of the word as it is read, preached, sung, prayed and displayed in the sacraments.

Consider an analogous situation. What if an athletic team competed in a sport in which their practices were allowed only one day per week. The other six days private workouts or position trainings were allowed (say, all the wide receivers were allowed to train together), yet the team as a team was allowed but one day to train together, to coordinate strategy, perfect tactics, and review its plays. Would we think that the one day was crucial? Would we think that it was vital for the sake of personal and team success that everyone be present? Would it not be obvious that the one day had a crucial role to play in the success of each player and the team as a whole?

This may be an answer to those who lament that they have not grown spiritually as they wish they had over the previous weeks, or months, or years, or even decades. A careful Sabbath would have had them laying aside all distracting secular activity, placed them in church with God's people Sunday morning and Sunday evening, and afforded them the time during the remainder of the day to pray and read Scripture privately and with their families. This could not but have made a difference, if these devotional exercises were entered into willingly and with sincerity. The logic of the Sabbath commandment requires us to understand the pivotal role that the day of worship and rest plays in our spiritual growth and development.

This may be an answer as well for those who lament the impotence of the church since the mid-twentieth century. The gathering of the whole church and all churches Sunday morning and evening, offering its public sacrifice of praise and devoting the remainder of the day to 'holy rest' could not but have strengthened the church against the secular onslaught of recent decades. Previous generations also understood this relationship between the church's impact and the Christian Sabbath. For example, Thomas Brooks, preaching in the aftermath of the Great Fire of London in 1666, affirmed,

> The true reason why the power of godliness is fallen to so low an ebb, both in this and in other countries also, is because the Sabbath is no more strictly and conscientiously observed in this land, and in those other countries where the name of the Lord is made known.[48]

The Sabbath has a vital role to play in preserving, protecting, and strengthening the whole believing community. The logic of the Sabbath commandment requires us to understand this. These are matters for us to ponder and upon which to act. We ignore the logic of the fourth commandment, of the Christian Sabbath, of the Lord's Day itself, to our peril.

Some claim that Jesus and the apostles set aside the Sabbath command altogether, freeing Christians from the obligation to devote a day to the worship and service of God. This, we argue, is fundamentally to misunderstand Jesus' ministry. He did not abolish even a 'jot and tittle' of the Old Testament law. Rather, he maintained its normativity until 'heaven and earth pass away' (Matt. 5:17-20). Jesus constantly was cutting a path between the profane looseness of the Pharisees on some matters and their superstitious strictness on others (see Matt. 5:21-48; 15:1-28; 23:16-28). Repeatedly, he demonstrated that doing good and preserving life on the Sabbath was not forbidden (Matt. 12:1-12; Mark 2:23–3:4; Luke 6:1-11; 13:10-17; John 5:1-18; 9:1-16). Nothing he said or did implies its abolition. He established that though the Christian Sabbath 'is under the direction of the fourth commandment,' says Henry, 'yet it is not under the arbitrary injunctions of the Jewish elders.'[49] He *is* 'Lord of the Sabbath,' not *was.*

---

[48] Brooks, 'London's Lamentations,' *Works*, VI:306.
[49] Henry, 'Serious Address,' *Works*, I:122.

What, then, are we to make of the apostle Paul's allowance that some will esteem one day above another and while others will not (Rom. 14:5, 6); that those who observe 'days, and months, and seasons and years' give evidence of being under law and not grace (Gal 4:9-11); and that no one should judge another with regard to 'a festival, a new moon, or a Sabbath' which he identifies as 'a shadow of things to come' (Col 2:16, 17)? The church's answer has been that we should understand the Apostle to be referring to the *Jewish* Sabbath with its extra-biblical regulations, as well as Judaism's calendar of holy days, that is the various other 'Sabbaths' in addition to the seventh day of the week. Commenting on Colossians 2:16, 17, Warfield maintains that the apostle 'does indeed sweep away with those words the whole system of typical ordinances' yet with 'no intention whatsoever of impairing … the obligations of the moral law.' As we have seen, Sabbath observance is a creation ordinance (Gen. 2:3), predates the ceremonial law (Exod. 16:23-28) and as the fourth of ten commandments is one of the 'Ten Words,' which alone in all the Bible were written by the finger of God on tablets of stone (Deut. 10:4). Warfield argues of the Ten Commandments as a whole, 'It is simply unimaginable that he could have allowed that any precept of this fundamental proclamation of essential morality could pass into desuetude.'[50]

All God's commands are 'for man.' All of them are for our good. They all promote human flourishing. They all provide the instructions of our Maker's operating manual for the human organism. They 'are not burdensome' (1 John 5:3). The laws of God are 'holy and just and good' (Rom. 7:12). The Sabbath command, Ryle and our spiritual forefathers would have us understand, 'is not a yoke, but a blessing. It is not a burden, but a mercy. It is not a hard wearisome

[50] Warfield, 'Foundations of the Sabbath,' *Selected Writings*, I:321; see also Durham, *Ten Commandments*, 162-63, 187.

requirement, but a mighty public benefit.'[51] Are we, then, to think that Christ acted so as to deprive humanity of that which is for its physical and spiritual good? Are we to think that in an era of a better covenant with better promises and greater blessings that he withdrew this good thing (Heb. 7:22; 8:6)? Were the Old Testament saints the beneficiaries of the institution of the Sabbath which the New Testament believers are now deprived? Does there not remain today a Sabbath rest for the people of God, one which anticipates their eternal rest with God in heaven (Heb. 4:1-9)?[52] If Jesus had abolished the Sabbath, it would have been a 'diminution, not an increase of the blessing given to the Jewish church,' said Jonathan Edward's grandson and President of Yale College, Timothy Dwight (1752–1817), voicing the outlook of our Christian past, and one can pray, our Christian future.[53]

---

[51] Ryle, 'Christian Sabbath,' *Knots Untied*, 342.

[52] Dabney: 'as there remains to believers under the Christian dispensation a hope of an eternal rest, so there remains to us an earthly Sabbath to foreshadow it' ('Christian Sabbath,' *Discussions*, I:535).

[53] Iain H. Murray, *Jonathan Edwards: A New Biography* (Edinburgh: Banner of Truth Trust, 1987), 84; If the Sabbath were abrogated, it would mean that 'the new dispensation is less blessed than the old' (Dabney, 'Christian Sabbath,' *Discussions*, I:524); John Murray adds this: Jesus is Lord of the Sabbath, 'not for the purpose of depriving men of that inestimable benefit which the Sabbath bestows, but for the purpose of bringing to the fullest realization on behalf of men that beneficent design for which the Sabbath was instituted' ('The Moral Law and the Fourth Commandment,' in *Collected Writings of John Murray* [Edinburgh: Banner of Truth Trust, 1976], I:208).

LORD OF THE SABBATH

Mark 2:28–3:5

There are two comprehensive principles governing the Christian Sabbath. First, Jesus teaches us that 'the Sabbath was made for man' (Mark 2:27). It was given by God for the benefit of humanity in the Garden of Eden prior to the fall. His pattern of six days of labour and a day of rest was to be our own pattern. This principle of rest was later codified in the fourth of the Ten Commandments (Exod. 20:8-11). The Sabbath, the Lord's Day (Rev. 1:10), is for our good, for our benefit, both physically (as rest) and spiritually (as worship). This brings us now to the second comprehensive principle. Christ Jesus is 'Lord of the Sabbath.'

Lord of the Sabbath

'So the Son of Man is lord even of the Sabbath' (Mark 2:28).

The Sabbath is 'for man,' yet it is not up to man to decide what he *will* do or *won't do* on it. It is 'for man,' but the Son of Man is its Lord. It is the Lord's Day (Rev. 1:10). It is his day, not ours. He determines what is permitted and what isn't. He decides what is approved and what isn't. He commands what is allowed, what is suitable, what is obligatory, what is appropriate, what is edifying, and what isn't. While it has become common in some circles to think of Sunday as a 'family day,' or golf day, or a day to relax, this is incorrect. Sunday is the Lord's Day, a point which Isaiah makes emphatic.

If you turn back your foot from the Sabbath, from doing your pleasure on my holy day, and call the Sabbath a delight and the holy day of the LORD honourable; if you honour it, not going your own ways, or seeking your own pleasure, or talking idly; then you shall take delight in the LORD, and I will make you ride on the heights of the earth; I will feed you with the heritage of Jacob your father, for the mouth of the LORD has spoken' (Isa. 58:13, 14).

God through Isaiah speaks of '*your own* pleasure' and '*your own* ways' and even 'talking idly.' There are sinful *pleasures* and sinful *ways* and sinful *words* that always are forbidden. However, those are not what is in view. Rather, what is being targeted is pleasures, ways, and words that otherwise would be permitted, but are not simply because it is the Sabbath. The day is to be dedicated not to *our own*, but to God's *pleasures, ways*, and *words*. Even so, it is still a 'delight' because one finds 'delight *in the Lord*' (Isa. 58:13, 14). It is *his* day. Therefore, *he* determines its activities.

So far we have emphasized that secular work is not an option on the Lord's Day. 'Six days you shall labour and do *all your* work' (Exod. 20:9). I must quit working on Sundays. If I don't quit working, I am guilty of breaking his command. If my job requires that I work on Sunday, I should explore the possibility of different work. Similarly, I must quit hiring others. Every time I employ someone to serve me, I violate the Sabbath over which Jesus Christ is Lord.

Beyond this, the day must be kept holy. This means that I should not allow myself to get caught up in *any* worldly or secular concerns that distract me from the things of God. I should never allow myself to miss Sunday worship because of worldly activity. It is wise to cancel the Sunday paper, to turn off the television, to minimize the use of the smart phone (avoiding everything except interpersonal communication). Why? Because all such distractions undermine the rest and refreshment of the soul that the Lord's Day is meant to promote. If for some this sounds strict to the point of legalism, we may remind ourselves that it is not legalism to obey God, whether we are dealing with the Fourth Commandment or the Sixth.[54] Because the Sabbath is 'for man' does not make it a free-for-all, each one doing what is right in his or her own eyes. We are free to 'do good' and 'save life' (Mark 3:4), yet it is still uniquely his day and he its Lord. Unless one is willing to argue that Christ is Lord of an institution which no longer exists, it necessarily means that he is uniquely Lord of my Sunday. It is not mine. It is his. I must do and not do as he says, no more and no less.

So while there is room for leisure (e.g. outdoor activity, moderate exercise), the leisure of Sunday is not the leisure of Monday through Saturday. The *Confession* and catechisms prohibit '*worldly* employments and recreations,' not *sanctified* employments and recreations (*WCF* XXI.7; *SC* Questions 60, 61; *LC* Questions 117,

[54] B. B. Warfield made this point about as well as it can be said: 'I am to recall your minds—it may seem somewhat brusquely—to the contemplation of the duty of the Sabbath; and to ask you to let them rest for a moment on the bald notion of authority. I do not admit that, in so doing, I am asking you to lower your eyes. Rather, I conceive myself to be inviting you to raise them; to raise them to the very pinnacle of the pinnacle. After all is said, there is no greater word than 'ought.' And there is no higher reason for keeping the Sabbath than that I ought to keep it; that I owe it to God the Lord to keep it in accordance with his command' (B. B. Warfield, 'Foundations of the Sabbath' in *Selected Writings*, I:308); Murray adds: 'Why should insistence upon Sabbath observance be pharisaical or legalistic? The question is: Is it a divine ordinance? If it is, then adherence to it is not legalistic any more than adherence to the other commandments of God. Are we to be charged with legalism if we are meticulously honest? If we are jealous not to deprive our neighbour unjustly of one penny which is his, and are therefore meticulous in the details of money transactions, are we necessarily legalistic? ... Are we to be charged with legalism if we are scrupulously chaste and condemn the very suggestions or gesture of lewdness? How distorted our conception of the Christian ethic and of the demands of holiness has become if we associate concern for the details of integrity with pharisaism and legalism!' (Murray, 'Moral Law,' *Collected Writings*, I:214).

119).[55] Sunday's leisure is to be undertaken directly, consciously, even obviously to promote my love for God and his works. Sunday leisure is to be undertaken with what previous generations called 'Sabbath restraint' and what the Puritan Thomas Case (1598–1682) called 'Sabbath affections.'[56] Our generation has made an idol of recreation to the great detriment of the public ministry of the Church. Scores of our people are missing from services each Sunday because of the god of leisure. This is wrong. Sunday is not *my* day. It is *the Lord's Day*, which he regulates for our benefit both physically and spiritually. We are not to take this good thing which he has given to us and create our own rules and twist it to our own ends. Our rest is to be a holy rest. Our worship is to be a holy worship. Our leisure is to be a holy leisure. All Sunday activity is to promote my love and appreciation for God and his works because it is his day, and he commands that we keep it holy.

A helpful question to ask of our Sunday activities is this: do they enhance my appreciation of God and his work? Certainly attending the morning and evening services do. So also does participating in Sunday School. Likewise does reading Christian books, reading the Bible, and listening to Christian sermons and lectures. As families we can enjoy times of singing and prayer and fellowship.

Certain leisure activities, what Ryle calls 'lawful relaxation' for the body, also can promote an appreciation of God and his creation.[57] Strolls in the park and along the seashore, outdoor picnics, and other similar activities can promote love and appreciation for God and his works. 'I am no admirer of a gloomy religion,' Ryle insists. Sunday, he maintains, should be 'the brightest, cheerfulest day of

[55] Non-worldly 'employments' are elaborated in terms of the works of necessity and mercy by the *Confession* and catechisms. Non-worldly recreations are not specified.

[56] Case, 'Sabbath Sanctification,' in *Puritan Sermons*, II:33.

[57] Ryle, 'Christian Sabbath,' *Knots Untied*, 347.

all the seven.'[58] There is considerable room for freedom here, but within these parameters.

On the other hand, I should ask myself, do any of my Sunday activities distract my attention from the things of God and take my heart elsewhere? If so, such endeavours should be studiously avoided lest I lose the blessing of the day.

Are there reasonable exceptions to the 'no work' rule? Indeed. When there is a particular human need which is crying out to be met, we should meet it. The Sabbath *blessing* is not to become a *curse* by the refusal to do certain necessary works, or meet certain basic needs. Neither are we to so construe the 'don'ts' of the Sabbath that our outlook primarily is negative. One may be overly strict as well as overly lenient. Owen complains of those whose list of duties that are necessary for the sanctification of the Lord's Day that 'a man can scarcely in six days read over all the duties that are proposed to be observed on the seventh.'[59] As in all of life, proper biblical proportions are crucial. The human heart, as Shepard argues, 'is apt to run to extremes, either to gross profaneness or pharisaical strictness.' Consequently, it is necessary to consider the question what is and what is not allowed on the Sabbath.[60] 'We must receive and embrace it as a privilege and a benefit,' says Henry, 'not as a task and a drudgery.'[61] Those who violate its principles 'do a great dishonour to God,' Henry reminds us, 'and no less *an injury to themselves.*'[62] What, then, are the works which the Sabbath command accommodates?

[58] *Ibid.*, 348.
[59] Owen, 'Exercitations Concerning a Day of Sacred Rest,' *Hebrews*, III:441.
[60] Shepard, *Theses Sabbaticae*, III:257.
[61] Henry, *Exposition*, on Mark 2:27.
[62] Henry, 'Serious Address,' *Works*, I:123 (emphasis added).

One Sabbath he was going through the grainfields, and as
they made their way, his disciples began to pluck heads of
grain. And the Pharisees were saying to him, 'Look, why are
they doing what is not lawful on the Sabbath?' And he said to
them, 'Have you never read what David did, when he was in
need and was hungry, he and those who were with him: how
he entered the house of God, in the time of Abiathar the high
priest, and ate the bread of the Presence, which it is not lawful
for any but the priests to eat, and also gave it to those who were
with him?' (Mark 2:23-26).

The disciples are walking through grain fields. They are hungry.
The law permits them to pluck grain by hand from one's neighbour's
fields (Deut. 23:25). However, it does not allow one to reap on the
Sabbath (Exod. 34:21). That would be work. Is plucking by hand
for personal needs the same as reaping? Is it work and a violation
of the fourth commandment?

Jesus answers by citing the example of David in 1 Samuel 21:1-6.
Twelve fresh loaves of bread were placed on a table before the Holy
of Holies each day. Only the priests were allowed to eat them after
they were removed (Lev 24:5-9). However, Jesus declares that this
restriction only applied under normal circumstances. David and his
men ate the bread when they were hungry and there was no other
bread available to them, and they were 'guiltless' or 'innocent' (Matt.
12:5, NASB). Why? Because basic human need takes precedence over
ceremonial design. In Matthew's account, Jesus cites Hosea 6:6: 'I
desire mercy and not sacrifice' (Matt. 12:7). 'Sacrifice' is ceremonial,
'mercy' is moral.

How, then, does this incident inform our understanding of Sabbath observance? The bread was for the priests' benefit. However,
they may relax the ceremonial restriction, share that blessing and

forfeit their enjoyment of the bread when a human need is involved. What was designed for the well-being of the body must not be interpreted as forbidding, as Henry says, 'in a case of necessity, from fetching in the necessary *supports* of the body.' Again, the fourth commandment 'must be construed so as not to contradict itself.'[63] It is *for* man. Don't construe it in such a way as *harms* man. Similarly, we not only *may*, but *must*, forfeit our blessing of rest when a human need is involved. It is 'lawful,' says Jesus to 'do good' and 'save life' (Mark 3:4). 'Whatever, in short, is necessary to preserve and maintain life, whether of ourselves, or of the creatures, or to do good to the souls of men, may be done on the Sabbath day without sin,' Ryle insists.[64] Traditionally this principle has led to the identification of works of necessity, mercy, and piety.[65]

Works of necessity

May soldiers work (fight) on Sunday? It is alleged that the Roman commander Pompey (106–48 BC) was able to conquer Jerusalem on a Sabbath day because zealous Jews refused to fight, lest they desecrate it. We know that the issue of whether to fight on the Sabbath or not to fight was long disputed among the Jews. The principle Jesus invokes resolves the debate. Military defence should be seen as a necessary work—to 'save life.' The refusal of an army to fight would subject a civilian population to enormous suffering and death. Similarly, the police may work. To allow Sunday to be a day of unrestrained criminal activity would not be 'good for man.'

[63] Henry, *Exposition,* on Mark 2:27.

[64] Ryle, 'Christian Sabbath,' *Knots Untied,* 346.

[65] The Westminster catechisms speak of two types of permitted works: those of necessity and mercy, to which the Westminster Seminary professor John Murray added a third, for the purposes of clarification, that of piety (see Joseph A. Pipa, *The Lord's Day* [Fearn, Ross-shire: Christian Focus, 1997], 78); Murray, 'The Sabbath Institution,' *Collected Writings,* I:213; the three-fold distinction was found previously in Durham, *Ten Commandments,* 214ff.

Pilots may guide their ships. Firefighters may work. Power company employees may work and spare the populace needless suffering.[66] So may those who make provision for the needs of travellers. Guests in our community need not sleep in their cars or on the streets. We may prepare and serve meals. One need not to be subjected to hunger pains because it is Sunday. Cows may even be milked, livestock may be fed, diapers may be changed. There are a number of these sorts of works which are necessary for the orderly living of life, and cannot be avoided and should not be avoided. One may make the bed, wash and groom oneself, hang up one's clothing, turn off the lights, drive the car, defend oneself and one's family from harm, and discipline the children.[67] Necessity, then, does not mean absolute necessity. One could abstain from eating and not suffer harm from twenty-four hours of fasting. Rather, necessity includes that which is necessary for the comfort of life.

We list these mainly because of the kinds of objections or alleged inconsistencies that are raised to Sabbath observance. Some take an area of grey as a rationale to give up the whole endeavour. This is foolish. The Sabbath is a day of rest, but *only* from those works which are *not* necessary. As much as I may dislike having to shave, I may still 'work' to get myself clean-faced on Sunday morning. One might think, well, if I still have to care for the children and prepare meals, it's not much of a rest. That may be true, but it is better than no rest at all, and we are not to despise the day of small things or despise the rest we do get because of the rest we don't. Even so, these 'necessary' works should be reduced to a minimum.

[66] Shepard even includes 'keep(ing) fire in the iron mills' (*Theses Sabaticae*, III:257).

[67] Durham refers to these as 'works of comeliness' including 'putting on of clothes, making the house clean from any uncleanliness, etc.' (*Ten Commandments*, 210); also Shepard, *Theses Sabaticae*, III:259. Similarly, Boston labels these 'works of decency' (*Shorter Catechism*, II:195).

The house does not need to be spotless or perfectly neat. Meals can be prepared the day before and should be as simple as practical. One who is in the kitchen daily cooking and cleaning may need a sandwich and a paper plate break!

At the same time we should be careful not to interpret the category of 'necessity' too broadly. It 'ought not to be a self-created necessity,' Henry wisely warns.[68] At times what we think is a necessity actually may not be. The United States has been without a President for a full day twice in our history. When James Polk left office in 1849, Zachary Taylor refused to be installed on Sunday. The same occurred again in 1877 when Ulysses S. Grant and Rutherford B. Hayes were the participants. Observing the Lord's Day was more important to Taylor and Hayes than assuming the office of the Presidency. The installation could wait for Monday! In a word, it is 'lawful on the Sabbath to do good' (Mark 3:4). We may do those things which are necessary, truly necessary, for the orderly living of life and the neglect of which would cause unnecessary hardship.

Works of mercy

> Again he entered the synagogue, and a man was there with a withered hand. And they watched Jesus, to see whether he would heal him on the Sabbath, so that they might accuse him. And he said to the man with the withered hand, 'Come here.' And he said to them, 'Is it lawful on the Sabbath to do good or to do harm, to save life or to kill?' (Mark 3:1-4).

Jesus heals on the Sabbath because it is lawful to do good and save life. The Pharisees would allow medical care only if the life was truly endangered. They would not, for example, allow a fracture or sprain to be treated. If a finger was cut, it could be bandaged, but

---

[68] Henry, 'Serious Address,' *Works*, I:120; see also Durham, *Ten Commandments*, 211; Boston, *Shorter Catechism*, II:195.

no ointment could be applied. One was only to do as much 'work' as was necessary to keep an injury from getting worse, and no more. The legislation was quite explicit.

> And he looked around at them with anger, grieved at their hardness of heart, and said to the man, 'Stretch out your hand.' He stretched it out, and his hand was restored (Mark 3:5).

Jesus is angered and 'grieved,' the latter word indicating deep internal grief and anguish, because of the complete insensitivity and hard-heartedness of the Pharisees. 'They watched Jesus, to see … so that they might accuse him' (Mark 3:2). They deliberately set out to trap him when the issue is not some great theological or moral issue, but whether or not he will help a handicapped man. In Matthew's parallel, Jesus exposes their inconsistency, even their cruelty by asking if they wouldn't do as much for a sheep if it fell in a pit (they would and did), and yet they objected to relieving human suffering (Matt. 12:11, 12).

Rest is not the ultimate goal of the Sabbath day, as we have seen. Rest is the means to the greater end of human benefit, both physical and especially spiritual. This benefit normally would include physical rest, but not at the expense of medical needs left unattended and suffering unrelieved. Disaster would ensue if doctors, nurses, pharmacists, and all other medical personnel insisted on Sunday rest. Sunday would become a curse rather than a blessing for many. It is lawful for all medical personnel to do good and relieve human suffering. Medical needs take precedence over our rest.

We should include in the 'mercy' category those who respond to emergency needs, whether professionals or not. I need not ever worry about whether or not to help a stranded motorist on Sunday. Such help would be a work of mercy. Whenever we confront hurting, suffering, needful people, we are obliged to help, whether it is the Christian Sabbath or not.

Our duties in this regard are not just passive (i.e., if an injured pedestrian should cross our path), but active. Sunday is a day for seeking out works of mercy, of visiting shut-ins, nursing homes, and hospitals. It is a day for helping the poor, working in soup kitchens, and crisis pregnancy centres. It is lawful to do good!

Works of piety

In Matthew's parallel Jesus elaborates what we might have guessed was the case. The priests in the temple 'profane the Sabbath and are guiltless' (Matt. 12:5-7). *Profane* should be understood as within quotation marks, meaning 'profane' as some might understand it. Yet in truth the priests are not profaning it at all, but are *guiltless*. They are *working*, but it is necessary work in relation to the tasks of the temple. Ministers, Sunday School teachers, elders, deacons, musicians, singers, and all those connected with the services of the church such as nursery workers and kitchen and custodial help, are permitted to work.

These three categories of work illustrate our point made earlier that the 'rest' of the Sabbath is not 'inactivity.' Rather, it requires the cessation of our daily secular labour so that we may take up religious work. We are to take up that which is for the good and benefit of ourselves and others. This includes rest and relaxation. Yet it also means ministry: worship, Bible study, visiting the sick, helping the needy, doing whatever the Lord gives us to do that will promote the physical and spiritual well-being of ourselves and others.

Christ and Sabbath focus

It remains for us to emphasize one additional principle. Jesus not only is Lord of the Sabbath, but also its focus and content. Jesus invites one and all:

Come to me, all who labour and are heavy laden, and I will give you rest. Take my yoke upon you, and learn from me, for I am gentle and lowly in heart, and you will find rest for your souls. For my yoke is easy, and my burden is light (Matt. 11:28-30).

'Rest' is a metaphor of redemption. We may speak of salvation as ransom price paid (Mark 10:45) or drinking living water (John 4:10) or eating the bread of life (John 6:35), and in each case represent a perspective on salvation. So also *rest*.

When describing salvation as rest, Jesus was utilizing an Old Testament concept. Psalm 95 speaks of the people of God entering into God's rest, in this case the promised land, or failing to do so because of unbelief (Psa. 95:11; cf. Heb. 3:7-19). The Letter to the Hebrews presents the promise of heavenly rest in the present tense. 'The promise of entering his rest still stands' (Heb. 4:1). The Christian Sabbath is meant to serve as a foretaste of eternal rest with God in heaven. It is 'the dawning of the heavenly Sabbath,' says Watson.[69] Through Christ Jesus we enter into that rest, which in this world is partial and imperfect, but then will be perfected. The Christian Sabbath anticipates the consummation of that rest. So again, the writer to the Hebrews says, 'So then, there remains a Sabbath rest for the people of God' (Heb. 4:9).

There 'remains' *now*, in the present era, a 'Sabbath rest' for believers that foreshadows our heavenly rest. Thomas Shepard writes inspiringly of the rest that the believer has in Christ of which the Christian Sabbath is a token and pledge. Holy duties are to be pursued 'that one may find and feel the sweet of the true rest of

[69] Watson, *Ten Commandments*, 118. It is, says Flavel, 'an emblem of that eternal Sabbath in heaven' ('Exposition,' *Works,* VI:233); Murray: 'The weekly Sabbath is the promise, token, and foretaste of the consummated rest; it is also the earnest' ('The Pattern of the Lord's Day,' *Collected Writings,* I:224); Owen, 'Exercitations Concerning a Day of Sacred Rest,' *Hebrews,* III:447-49.

the Sabbath' found in 'such a fruition of God as gives rest to our souls.'[70] That rest finds its perfection in heaven but it begins here. God has fixed a day 'that the weary man may enjoy his rest, his God, his love, his heaven … in this life, until he come up to glory, to rest with God.' Days of glory come later. Yet believers through the Spirit 'may foretaste them in days of grace.'[71] That greater rest remains ahead of us. Yet on Sundays we celebrate the rest that is ours in Christ *now* even as we look forward to our completed rest *then*. Our Christian Sabbath is 'a little prelude of that everlasting Sabbath and rest in the bosom of God,' says Durham.[72]

---

[70] Shepard, *Theses Sabbaticae*, III:263-64.

[71] *Ibid.*, 266.

[72] Durham, *Ten Commandments*, 217.

PRACTICAL RECOMMENDATIONS

All that we have reviewed to this point adds up to a marvellous institution for the church and society, the loss of which has hurt us all. It has hurt us physically and spiritually, depriving us of rest and impoverishing our souls. It has distracted us further from taking up works of mercy and piety. The larger society has been harmed by the loss of its Sabbath rest as the work week has expanded and forced many into Sunday labour. The Lord's Day is the day that he particularly has blessed (Exod. 20:11). It is the day that he particularly urges us to seek him, and consequently, the day in which he is most likely to be found.

What can we do to bring back a healthy, biblical Sabbatarianism, meaning biblical observance of the Sabbath, as it was meant to be observed, avoiding on the one hand the pitfalls of the legalists, and on the other, of the libertines? Proper observance will require a certain degree of preparation and prior planning. The *Westminster Confession of Faith* urges a 'due preparing' of our hearts and 'ordering of (our) common affairs beforehand' (XXIII.8).[73] Brooks, typical of the classic authors, urges, 'To holy performances there ought to be holy preparations.'[74] We offer the following recommendations.

---

[73] *Larger Catechism*, Q. 117, adds, 'To that end, we are to prepare our hearts, and with such foresight, diligence, and moderation, to dispose and seasonably dispatch our worldly business, that we may be the more free and fit for the duties of that day.'(see also *Shorter Catechism*, Q. 60).

[74] Brooks, 'London's Lamentations,' *Works*, VI:288; see also Watson, *Ten Commandments*, 101-07; Durham, *Ten Commandments*, 218ff; Boston, *Shorter Catechism*, II:197, 203.

Prepare spiritually

Begin to prepare for the Lord's Day on Saturday night. During family devotions, we may ask God to prepare our hearts to meet with him on Sunday. Through reading Scripture and prayer one may bring one's heart into what Watson calls a 'Sabbath-frame.'[75] Develop a sense of anticipation and joy for this greatest of times on the greatest of days. Sunday is the day that we meet with our God, Father, Son, and Holy Spirit, and enjoy his fellowship. Sunday, the day in which the people of God gather for worship, is the day that Jesus promises to be present with his people (Matt. 18:20). Sunday is the day in which we rejoice together recalling the great works of God in creation, providence, and redemption. Prepare for this by spending time in prayer, confessing sin, reading his word, asking God to bless the day, its services, and especially the preaching.

Plan to devote the time outside of congregational worship to consecrated rest, which as we have seen means anything from naps to reading the Bible or Christian books, to hospital visits or strolls in the park. Plan for these things. If preparation is not made, one may end up doing none of these things and instead doing nothing or succumbing to the temptation to take up worldly activities. This is where a Sunday evening worship service helps. The Christian Sabbath and Sunday night church are mutually helpful. Psalm 92 provides 'both a precept and platform for Sabbath sanctification,' says Case.[76] According to its superscription, Psalm 92 is 'A Song for the Sabbath.' It envisions the faithful declaring God's 'steadfast love in the *morning,* and (his) faithfulness by *night*' (Psa. 92:2). The practice of morning and evening sacrifice established the pattern of morning and evening prayer for the people of God, at least since the time of Moses (see Psa. 5:3 and 141:2). It has prevailed ever since,

---

[75] Watson, *Ten Commandments*, 105.

[76] Case, 'Sabbath Sanctification,' in *Puritan Sermons*, II:29.

or at least until recent decades. The Lord's Day in this context may develop a natural rhythm. One may move throughout the day from Sunday School to morning worship, to Sunday dinner at home, to a few hours of afternoon rest, returning to the church for evening worship, and afterwards a fellowship supper. By the time one returns home, the day is all but over, having been filled from top to bottom with worship, fellowship, and rest.

Conclude common affairs

If we are to be successful in devoting ourselves to the things of God, we must draw our common activities to a close by Saturday evening. Learn to get all work-week activity done in six days. 'Six days you shall labour and do all your work.' Impossible? It is a truism that work tends to expand to fill whatever space and time we allow. This is why many of us ended up finishing our term papers the night before they were due, though we knew for weeks or even months when they were due. This is the case of every kind of work. Eliminating a day forces us to plan better and rest better. 'The gift of the Sabbath,' says Sinclair Ferguson, 'provided a wonderful way of regulating the whole of life.'[77] Eliminate Sunday as a day of work first, and it will help to discipline our use of time in the rest of the week. If the twenty-four hours of the Lord's Day are not available to us, we will become more efficient in our use of the twenty-four hours of the other six days. We are to redeem the time, says J. I.

[77] Ferguson, *Devoted to God*, 266; see also Durham, *Ten Commandments*, 221-23. Megachurch pastor John Mark Comer observes, 'But Sabbath is more than just a day; it's a way of being in the world. It is a spirit of restfulness that comes from abiding, from living in the Father's loving presence all week long (*Ruthless Elimination of Hurry*, 45). He cites an Old Testament theologian: '"People who keep sabbath live all seven days differently." It's true. Watch out for the Sabbath. It will mess with you. First it will mess with one day of your week; then it will mess with your whole life' (*Ibid.*, 150).

Packer in his comments on the Christian Sabbath,

> not by a frenzied rushing to pack a quart of activity into a
> pint of time (a common present-day error), but by an ordered
> lifestyle in which, within the set rhythm of toil and rest, work
> and worship, due time is allotted to sleep, family, wage earning,
> homemaking, prayer, recreation and so on, so that we master
> time, instead of being mastered by it.[78]

Sabbath observance has a role to play in bringing order to our
lives. We must be diligent 'to dispose and dispatch our worldly business,' says the *Larger Catechism*, 'that we may be the more free and fit
for the duties of the day' (Q. 117). What cannot be completed in six
days, assign to the next Monday. We also may prepare by getting to
bed early Saturday night. One might wind down by 10 p.m. and be
in bed by 11 p.m. Case complained in his day of 'people loading the
Saturday night with so many worldly affairs,' and as a consequence,
not arriving at church until the service was half over.[79] Worldlings
may be out all night Saturday, but we should not be. We're going
to meet with God, and for this we must be rested and alert.

In order to avoid working and employing others, shopping should
be completed by Saturday, the house cleaned, the gas tank filled, and
even the meals prepared the night before. Get all everyday activity
out of the way so that the rest may be as full as possible. Make all
purchases and complete all material preparation with a little extra for
potential guests, before Sunday. With a little effort and forethought,
this easily can be accomplished.

Persevere

A major problem that we face in our endeavours to re-establish
careful Sabbath observance is our underdeveloped appetite for

---

[78] J. I. Packer, *I Want to Be a Christian* (Eastbourne: Kingsway, 1977), 213.
[79] Case, 'Sabbath Sanctification,' *Puritan Sermons*, II:42.

spiritual things. The Old Testament prophets recognize the problem and denounce it. 'What a weariness this is,' the people complained of God's requirements (Mal. 1:13). 'When will the (Sabbath day) be over that we might sell again?' they impatiently asked (Amos 8:5). They had no interest in or capacity for spiritual things. Far too typically we too are drawn more to carnal and worldly excitements rather than to the more quiet and contemplative pleasures to be found in the things of God. We've heard complaints from some that they spend so much time at the church that Sunday is 'not restful' for them. They are worn out by the activities of the church, they say. We should concede that the church may burden its members with extraneous Sunday activities beyond the morning and evening worship services. Care should be taken by church leaders not to overwhelm its people. On the other hand, perhaps expectations need to be adjusted. It is not unusual to hear that some souls are worn out by three hours at church on Sunday, yet think nothing of spending hours and hours on Saturday driving, tailgating, eating, drinking, rooting for the home team, and celebrating victory or mourning defeat into the late hours. Their weekends are filled with work, youth sports, recitals, and travel. Of course they are weary on Sunday. Of course the church's calendar seems only to add to their already frenetic pace. Yet exhaustion from weekend recreation should never become an excuse for neglecting Lords' Day devotion. Perhaps we have erred in glorifying the Sunday afternoon nap to the point that the importance of the holy work of the Sabbath has been lost. The pace maintained from Monday through Saturday should take into account the sacred tasks of Sunday.

It is because we suffer from a reduced capacity for spiritual things that we tire so quickly.[80] Consequently, it is vital that we persevere

---

[80] On one occasion when the Westminster Assembly observed a day of prayer, they alternated preaching and praying for eight hours, six of which were spent in prayer!

in observing the Lord's Day, thereby providing time for our spiritual desires to mature. Before long we may find ourselves 'so well-employed, and so well entertained by (our) religion,' says Henry, 'that (we) will look with a holy contempt upon the employments and entertainments of the world.'[81] The promise of the prophet Isaiah may be fulfilled: we may call the Sabbath a 'delight' (Isa. 58:13, 14).

As we mature, we may come to wish that every day were a Sabbath day. We may grow to *delight* in the word of God, finding it to be more desirable than gold and sweeter than honey (Psa. 19:10; 119:14, 16, 35, 47, 77, 143). We may grow to love God's word (Psa. 119:48, 97, 113, 163, 165), and rejoice in it (Psa. 119:111, 162). We may grow to *delight* in the people of God, 'the saints … the excellent ones' (Psa. 16:3). We may grow to hunger and thirst for the presence of God among the assembled people of God, even as a deer pants for the water brooks (Psa. 42:1, 2, 4; 63:1, 2). We may grow to see God's 'dwelling place' as 'lovely,' a place where we long, even faint to be (Psa. 84:1, 2, 10). Our appetites, our desires may so change that we may say that the 'one thing' that we want and seek is that we 'may dwell in the house of the Lord all the days of (our) lives' (Psa. 27:4, 7, 8). We may long to feed upon the bread of life (John 6:35), to quench our spiritual thirst with living water (John 4:10-15; 7:37, 38), and find in Christ rest for our souls (Matt. 11:28-30).

When our appetites and desires change, no one will be dragging us to worship Sunday morning or evening; rather, we will be saying with the psalmist, 'I was glad when they said to me, let us go up to the house of God' (Psa. 122:1). No one will be forcing us to read our Bible or read edifying Christian literature because we will be able to say with the psalmist, 'Oh how I love your law! It is my meditation all the day' (Psa. 119:97; 1:2). Persevere until the day comes that we are so transformed into the image of God that we delight in the things of God on the day of God.

---

[81] Henry, 'Serious Address,' *Works*, I:123.

CONCLUSION

Let us conclude with a plea, an exhortation, and a promise.

A Plea

First, let us recognize that we Christians are our own worst enemies. For generations our nation observed a Sabbath cycle of work and rest. Everyone, Christians and non-Christians, worked six days and rested on Sunday. This arrangement was greatly to the church's advantage. It was at least theoretically possible for the entire congregation to meet together on Sunday. Virtually everyone had the day off.

Today a significant percentage of our people cannot meet with us because of work requirements. Either regularly or periodically they must work. Every year it becomes increasingly difficult for congregations to gather together. Every year an increasing percentage of the national work force must work on Sunday. We are our own worst enemies because every time we buy or sell on Sunday we contribute to an employment chain which is becoming longer and larger. When we buy food, someone must sell it, another must serve it, another must prepare it, another must deliver it, etc.

Years ago the churches of one Southern town banded together to crusade against Sunday store openings. They managed to persuade every shop to close except one, the owner of a small grocery store. The final discussion with the grocer went like this: a pastor persuaded the grocer to close his store all day with the exception of one hour, which he steadfastly refused to give up. 'I don't understand.' 'Why not close all day?' asked the exasperated pastor. Then the merchant dropped his bombshell. 'I'll remain open just one hour, from 12:00 to 1:00.' The pastor nodded, and walked out in acknowledgment of defeat. Between 12:00 and 1:00 his church members, on their way home from church services, made the purchases which made it profitable for him to open his store, even if only for one hour.

If we find our loved ones taking jobs that require Sunday work, we have only ourselves to blame. Fewer and fewer jobs do not require it. Frequently we are contributing to the breakdown. The one positive step that we all can take to slow down or even reverse this trend is to stop employing others on Sunday, and stop making purchases. We have seen that the fourth commandment implies that it is of critical importance that the people of God have *a* day in which to gather. If everyone who calls himself a Christian in our society would do so, it might not be profitable for the stores to remain open and they might close, and a non-commercial Sunday would again become universal.

An Exhortation

Second, we turn our attention once more to those who lament that they have not grown spiritually as they had hoped. They may discern in themselves many indications of biblical ignorance and persistent character flaws. For years they may have remained on a spiritual plateau. If this pattern of non-growth has included neglect of a careful Sabbath observance, this neglect undoubtedly has been a factor in the failure to mature. It may not be the only factor. It may not be the most important factor. However, it will be a factor. As we have seen, this is the implication of the fourth commandment. A day devoted to the things of God is a key element in God's programme for spiritual well-being of his people. If over the months and years the hours of each Sabbath day had been sincerely devoted to the word, worship and people of God, week after week, that commitment most certainly would have led to substantial spiritual growth.

The older authors understood this. Case insists that 'there are no such Christians, for exemplary holiness, as those who are taken notice of to make conscience of sanctifying the Sabbath.'[82] Similarly, Brooks claimed, 'There are no Christians in all the world comparable to those, for the power of godliness and heights of grace, holiness, and communion with God, who are most strict, serious, studious, and conscientious in sanctifying of the Lord's day.'[83] If instead, those Sabbath hours were squandered, wasted on things the moth and rust destroy, we need not wonder why we languish. Our souls need and thrive on a holy day each week.

Moreover, let us be exhorted not to classify this command as of secondary or tertiary importance. There is a subtlety to Sabbath observance. When we think of the bold refusal of Olympic hero and missionary Eric Liddell (1902–45) to compete on Sunday in preparation for the 1924 Olympic Games, do we think of a legalist or, as the movie portrayed him, a deeply devoted man of God, the kind of man we might want our sons to grow up to be? Surely it is the latter. When asked if he were willing to compete in his strongest event in the Paris Olympics on Sunday afternoon, and in particular, was he willing to do so since he was told, in France the Sabbath ended at noon, he answered, 'My Sabbath lasts all day.'[84] The willingness of Liddell to dedicate one day of the week entirely to the Lord, even if it cost him the opportunity to compete in the Olympics, spoke of a life in which all seven days were his. Liddell, in fact, went on to be a missionary in China and died at the age of 43 in a Japanese prison camp, a martyr for the faith.

The subtlety of the Sabbath is this—Liddell was willing to give one day in seven because all seven were the Lord's. Sabbath obser-

[82] Case, 'Sabbath Sanctification,' *Puritan Sermons*, II:41.

[83] Brooks, 'London's Lamentations,' *Works*, VI:305-06; so also Durham, *Ten Commandments*, 225.

[84] See Duncan Hamilton, *For the Glory: Eric Liddell's Journey from Olympic Champion to Modern Martyr* (New York: Penguin Press, 2016).

vance is a sort of litmus test. Ryle insists that 'delight in the Lord's word, the Lord's service, the Lord's people, and the Lord's Day will always go together.'[85] In fact, the Old Testament can at times speak of a pattern of disobedience as a 'profaning' of the Sabbath because Sabbath observance had come to stand for the totality of which God requires of his people (cf. Isa. 56:1-8; Jer. 17:19-27; Ezek. 20:19-24; 22:8, 26; 23:38). Disobedience here reveals a persistent worldly rebelliousness against God's authority lurking beneath the surface in one's heart. A Sabbath day provides a break from the world, so that 'while our hands rest from the business of the world and an antidote to worldliness, our minds may rest from the cares of it, and so,' says Henry, '*we may be saved from the inordinate love of it.*'[86]

Is Jesus Christ the Lord of our lives? If he is, there will be a willingness to observe the day of which he is uniquely Lord and of which our souls are particularly needy, regardless of what one may have to give up and regardless of what anyone says, whether the Prince of Wales (as in the film's depiction of Liddell's case) or anyone else. Surrendering to Christ in this area, giving up one's own pursuits in order to submit to his, marks a milestone in one's Christian commitment. He is our Lord, and in observing the Sabbath we demonstrate his lordship with something more than words. 'The stream of all religion runs either deep or shallow,' Henry warns, 'according as the banks of the Sabbath are kept up or neglected.'[87]

Sabbath-keeping is emblematic of the 'muscular,' uncompromising Christianity that alone can conquer our foes in this generation—a Christianity that defies pragmatic considerations, that denies self, that makes tough, costly decisions. 'My advice to all Christians,' says Ryle, 'is to contend earnestly for the whole day against all enemies, both without and within.'[88]

[85] Ryle, 'Christian Sabbath,' *Knots Untied*, 353.

[86] Henry, 'Serious Address,' *Works*, I:129 (emphasis added).

[87] *Ibid.*, I:134.

[88] Ryle, 'Christian Sabbath,' *Knots Untied*, 334.

A Promise

Finally, we return to the promise in Isaiah 58:13, 14:

> If because of the Sabbath, you turn your foot from doing your own pleasure on my holy day, and call the Sabbath a delight, the holy day of the LORD honourable, and shall honour it, desisting from your own ways, from seeking your own pleasure, and speaking your own word, then you will take delight in the LORD, and I will make you ride on the heights of the earth; and I will feed you with the heritage of Jacob your father, for the mouth of the LORD has spoken (NASB).

The Sabbath is a 'delight.'[89] It is a day of rejoicing. The stone rejected has become the chief cornerstone, and hence, speaking of the resurrection, the psalmist exclaims, 'This is the day that the LORD has made; let us rejoice and be glad in it' (Psa. 118:24).[90] This joy, Murray clarifies, 'is a solemn, holy joy … a triumphant joy, filled with the raptures of adoration and praise.' It may be contrasted with both 'cold, hypocritical formalism,' and with 'secular jollity.'[91]

'The Sabbaths of the holy are the suburbs of heaven,' says Swinnock.[92] For Shepard, the Sabbath is the 'twilight and dawning of heaven.'[93] The older authors understood this so well. Edwards cites Isaiah 58:13, 14 and Hebrews 4:9-11 saying, 'It is a pleasant and joyful day … an image of the future heavenly rest of the church.' 'The Christian sabbath,' he insists, 'is one of the most precious enjoyments of the visible church.'[94] God promises to bless us, and bless our

---

[89] See Walter Chantry, *Call the Sabbath a Delight* (Edinburgh: Banner of Truth Trust, 1991); Henry, 'Serious Address,' *Works*, I:133.

[90] Psalm 118:24 often was cited by the classic authors as prophetic of the Christian Sabbath (e.g. Durham, *Ten Commandments*, 205; Boston, *Shorter Catechism*, II:192-93; Flavel, 'Exposition,' *Works*, VI:233-34).

[91] Murray, 'The Relevance of the Sabbath,' *Collected Writings*, I:228.

[92] Swinnock, 'Christian Man's Calling,' *Works*, I:241.

[93] Shepard, *Theses Sabbaticae*, 254; also Durham, *Ten Commandments*, 225.

[94] Edwards, 'Perpetuity and Change,' Sermon XV, in *Works*, I:101; On the

families, and bless our church if we will observe his Sabbath. True observers of the Lord's day are promised 'that God will abundantly manifest his gracious presence and multiply his spiritual blessings that day,' says Durham.[95] *Physically*, we will find rest for our weary bodies. We will find ourselves with more energy, more life, and more vigour. *Spiritually*, we will find refreshment for our weary souls. We will experience a greater exposure to spiritual things, become more attuned and aware of the things of God, and deepen our love and appreciation for Christ and his kingdom. The Christian Sabbath is for our good; and our good is to be found in observing it in the manner in which he prescribes for us.

---

other hand, Owen asks of those wearied by the Sabbath, as have many others, 'What would such persons do if they should ever come to heaven to be taken aside to all eternity to be with God alone, who think it a great bondage to be here diverted unto him for a day?' (Owen, 'Exercitations Concerning a Day of Sacred Rest,' *Hebrews*, III:451); The Sabbath is not a delight for those who 'savour not the things of God,' says Boston (*Shorter Catechism*, II:202); 'many are quite out of their element on the Lord's day' (II:199); cf Henry, 'Serious Address,' *Works*, I:133.

[95] Durham, *Ten Commandments*, 223.

THE SABBATH AND DELIGHT

Hail thou that art highly favoured of God, thou map of heaven, thou golden spot of the week, thou market-day of souls, thou daybreak of eternal brightness, thou queen of days, the Lord is with thee, blessed art thou among days ... All the graces triumph in thee, all the ordinances conspire to enrich thee; the Father ruleth thee, the Son rose upon thee, the Spirit hath overshadowed thee ... On thee light was created, the Holy Ghost descended, life hath been restored, Satan subdued, sin mortified, souls sanctified, the grave, death, and hell conquered. Oh how do men and women flutter up and down on the week-days, as the dove on the waters, and can find no rest for their souls, till they come to thee their ark, till thou put forth thy hand and take them in! Oh how do they sit under thy shadow with great delight, and find thy fruits sweet to their taste! On the mountings of mind, the ravishing happiness of heart, the solace of soul which on thee they enjoy in the blessed Saviour! Let all thine ordinances be clothed with power, and be effectual for the conversion and salvation of millions of souls; let thy name be great from the rising of the sun to the going down of the same. Finally, farewell sweet day, thou cream of time, thou epitome of eternity—thou heaven in a glass, thou first-fruits of a blessed and everlasting harvest.

George Swinnock

SELECTED BIBLIOGRAPHY

Barclay, William, *The Ten Commandments for Today* (Grand Rapids: William B. Eerdmans Publishing, 1973).

Beckwith, Roger T. and Wilfrid Stott, *The Christian Sunday: A Biblical and Historical Study* (Grand Rapids: Baker Book House, 1980).

Beeke, Joel and Mark Jones, *A Puritan Theology* (Grand Rapids: Reformation Heritage Books, 2012).

Boston, Thomas, *A Commentary on the Shorter Catechism,* Vol. I. (1773, 1853; Edmonton: Still Water Revival Books, 1993).

—*Human Nature in its Fourfold State* (1720; London: Banner of Truth Trust, 1964).

Bound, Nicholas, *The True Doctrine of the Sabbath* (1606, Dallas: Naphtali Press and Reformation Heritage Books, 2015).

Brooks, Thomas, 'London's Lamentations' in *The Works of Thomas Brooks*, Vol. VI (Edinburgh: Banner of Truth Trust, 1980).

Case, Thomas. 'Of Sabbath Sanctification,' in *Puritan Sermons*, 6 Vols (Wheaton: Richard Owen Roberts Publishers, 1981).

Chantry, Walter, *Call the Sabbath a Delight* (Edinburgh: Banner of Truth Trust, 1991).

Childs, Brevard S., *The Book of Exodus: A Critical, Theological Commentary*, Old Testament Library (Philadelphia: Westminster Press, 1974).

Comer, John Mark, *The Ruthless Eliminator of Hurry* (Colorado Springs: Water Brook, 2019).

Dabney, R. L., 'The Christian Sabbath: Its Nature, Design and Proper Observance,' in *Discussions: Evangelical and Theological*, 3 Vols (1892; London: Banner of Truth Trust, 1967).

Dennison, James T., *The Market Day of the Soul: The Puritan Doctrine of the Sabbath in England, 1532–1700* (Grand Rapids: Reformation Heritage Books, 2008).

Durham, James, *Practical Exposition the Ten Commandments* (1675; Dallas: Naphtali Press and Grand Rapids: Reformation Heritage Books, 2018).

Edwards, Jonathan, 'Perpetuity and Change of the Sabbath,' Sermons XIII-XV, *The Works of Jonathan Edwards,* Vol. II, (Edinburgh: Banner of Truth Trust, 1974).

Ferguson, Sinclair B., *Devoted to God: Blueprints for Sanctification*, (Edinburgh: Banner of Truth Trust, 2016).

Flavel, John, 'An Exposition of the Assembly's Catechism,' *The Works of John Flavel*, Vol. VI, (1820; London: Banner of Truth Trust, 1968).

Hamilton, Duncan, *For the Glory: Eric Liddell's Journey from Olympic Champion to Modern Martyr* (New York: Penguin Press, 2016).

Henry, Matthew, 'A Serious Address to Those that Profane the Lord's Day,' in *The Complete Works of Matthew Henry,* Vol. I & II (1855; Grand Rapids: Baker Books, 1979).

—*Exposition of the Old and New Testaments*, Vol. V: Matthew to John (London: James Nisbet & Co.).

Hodge, Charles, *Systematic Theology*, 3 Vols (1870–73; Grand Rapids: Eerdmans Publishing Co., 1981).

Murray, Iain H., *Jonathan Edwards: A New Biography* (Edinburgh: Banner of Truth Trust, 1987).

Murray, John, *Principles of Conduct* (London: Tyndale Press, 1957).

— 'The Moral Law and the Fourth Commandment,' in *Collected Writings of John Murray*, Vol. I (Edinburgh: Banner of Truth Trust, 1976).

—'The Pattern of the Lord's Day,' in *Collected Writings of John Murray*, Vol. I (Edinburgh: Banner of Truth Trust, 1976).

—'The Relevance of the Sabbath,' in *Collected Writings of John Murray*, Vol. I (Edinburgh: Banner of Truth Trust, 1976).

—'The Sabbath Institution,' in *Collected Writings of John Murray*, Vol. I (Edinburgh: Banner of Truth Trust, 1976).

Owen, John, 'Exercitations Concerning the Name, Origin, Nature, Use, and Continuance of a Day of Sacred Rest,' in *An Exposition of the Epistle to the Hebrews*, 7 Vols (1855; Grand Rapids: Baker Books, 1980).

Packer, J. I., *I Want to Be a Christian* (Eastbourne: Kingsway Publications, 1977).

Pipa, Joseph A., *The Lord's Day* (Fearn, Ross-shire: Christian Focus Publications, 1997).

Reilly, Rick, 'Let Us ~~Pray~~ Play,' *Sports Illustrated,* April 26, 2004.

Ryle, J. C., 'The Christian Sabbath,' in *Knots Untied: being Plain Statements on Disputed Points in Religion from an Evangelical Standpoint* (Edinburgh: Banner of Truth Trust, 2016).

Shaw, Jean, 'Six Flags Instead of Sunday School,' *Presbyterian Journal*, May 24, 1984.

Shepard, Thomas, *Theses Sabbaticae, The Works of Thomas Shepard,* Vol. III (Ligonier: Soli Deo Gloria Publications, 1992).

Swinnock, George, 'The Christian Man's Calling,' in *The Works of George Swinnock*, Vol. I (1868; Edinburgh: Banner of Truth Trust, 1992).

The Westminster Confession of Faith and Catechisms (Lawrenceville: Christian Education and Publications, 2007).

Vos, Geerhardus, *Biblical Theology* (Grand Rapids: Eerdmans Publishing Co., 1948).

Warfield, B. B., 'The Foundations of the Sabbath in the Word of God,' in *Selected Shorter Writings of Benjamin B. Warfield*, Vol. I (Phillipsburg: Presbyterian and Reformed Publishing, 1970).

Watson, Thomas, *The Ten Commandments*, (1692, 1890: London: Banner of Truth Trust, 1965).

BANNER *of* **TRUTH**

The Banner of Truth Trust originated in 1957 in London. The founders believed that much of the best literature of historic Christianity had been allowed to fall into oblivion and that, under God, its recovery could well lead not only to a strengthening of the church, but to true revival.

Interdenominational in vision, this publishing work is now international, and our lists include a number of contemporary authors, together with classics from the past. The translation of these books into many languages is encouraged.

A monthly magazine, *The Banner of Truth*, is also published, and further information about this, and all our other publications, may be found on our website, banneroftruth.org, or by contacting the offices below:

Head Office:
3 Murrayfield Road
Edinburgh
EH12 6EL
United Kingdom
Email: info@banneroftruth.co.uk

North America Office:
PO Box 621
Carlisle, PA 17013
United States of America
Email: info@banneroftruth.org